SECRET HISTORIES

ALSO BY CRAIG WATSON:

Drawing a Blank, Singing Horse Press, 1980
The Asks, Potes & Poets, 1982
Discipline, Burning Deck, 1986
0.10, Awede Press, 1986
After Calculus, Burning Deck, 1988
Unsuspended Animation, Paradigm Press, 1991
Picture of the Picture of the Image in the Glass, O Books, 1992
Drum, Abacus-Potes & Poets, 1993
Reason, Zasterle, 1998
Free Will, Roof, 2000
True News, Instance Press, 2002

SECRET HISTORIES

Craig Watson

Burning Deck / Anyart
Providence

Acknowledgments:

Some of these poems were first published in *First Intensity, Kiosk, Shearsman, 26,* and *New American Poetry.*

The publication of this book was made possible by generous gifts in memory of Toni Warren and by an anonymous donor.

Burning Deck Press is the Literature Program of ANYART: CONTEMPORARY ARTS CENTER, a tax-exempt (501c3), non-profit organization.

Cover image: the Vinland Map

for Franklin J. Watson, 1924-2000
and Mildred S. Watson, 1924-2006

CONTENTS

11 Steppe Work

27 (Pre)Science

35 Last Man Standing

61 Loose Canons

This must be how salvation feels after a while
—Bob Dylan

Steppe Work

A Bow Spends Its Life Trying to Be a Straight Line

1.   last world lost first
        all promises promise themselves
        [what nature doesn't want]
        nothing lives for its own sake

2.   war makes culture
        [empire begins at defense]
        your money [and] your life

3.   heaven's curse [scorched by water on water]
        steal to own [that uncompensated distance]
        ashes for ashes [Prester John at the gates of Qaraqorum]

4.   then swam into the tall grass
        singing memories alone together
        as if the dead would not mind
        this wind of loving immolation

5.   is to kill
        [without being]
        killed
        [each footstep]
        [breath]
        mistaken for all

6.   a bluish wolf
        fell in love with
        a fallow deer
        [the Great Khan]
        [a womb unavenged]

7.   to be human [the lying animal]
        to believe a soul [made of mud]
        to whisper ["I belong to no-body"]

8.   "You must have committed the worst of sins
        for God to have sent a punishment like me"

9.   now that we know each other
        [said the future to the past]
        let us consummate
        [this marriage of convenience]
        divine fiction and earthly consequence

10.   pledge allegiance
        [by incident or design]
        choose god or choose decency
        anon [at] large
        alive [ex] utero

11.   [staring at the sun]
        could not erase
        mask of closed eyes
        [a tax on every breath]

12.   savages live the life they choose
        [beasts postponed by words]

13.   horsemen dismount the apocalypse
        they live like idols in the cathedral of birds
        their moon rains naked pine needles
        their hymns rage [the milk of grammar]

14.   a generation by genocide
        to worship the boiled meat of heaven
        no companion [other than] shadow
        no whip [other than own] tail

15.   how could a child lose itself
        abandoned by the lawgivers
        their daughters are our daughters
        as worthless as knowledge

16.   [a visit to the hordes]
        "are they afraid to die or
        that they might not"
        [the same as every other song]

17.   "love thy barbarian"
        [as thyself]

18.   [thus] the world was cleansed
        by an ancient and alien people
        to whom the sky was a green tent and
        music the breath of selfless assassins

19.   trees became skeletons
        [a winter in winter]
        the city [sky without light]
        betrothed an endless army

20.   [as if] asleep
        in [god's] barren saddle
        [unforgiven]

21.   enter heaven through hole at top of sky
        count miles by horse deaths
        eat own fingers
        inflict every extreme

22.   a second life in disguise
        [a heart made of grass]
        [a knife made of silk]
        centuries irrigated by blood

23.   the one about a lonely girl [thrown]
        deep in the well [her father long gone]
        [imagined] riches preserved

24.   suddenly the world appears
        [between gratitude and debt]
        sunset's honor regained defeat
        [threatening to kill what cannot die]

25.   at the first sign of prosperity
        a messenger arrives
        across the yellow lake
        riding on pontoons
        of human skins

26.   eye of the storm
        [as in black of an "I"]
        sight's blister dis
        [-appears] [-appoints]

27.   shamans in threes [human bombs]
        we paid full price to see one whole
        [truth-as-boundless] property

28.   [tied to poison arrow]
        "killed two wives by accident"
        [engraved on headstone]
        "suffered fulfillment in remnants"
        [shape-shifted on cloud silk]

29.   what they stole they stroked
        [lung by day] [heart by night]
        marriage [as much as war permits]

30.   [us] [them] onward
        [unborn]

31.   own devices [abandoned]
        ten thousand eyeless gods [ravished]
        how could we be so mistaken [gorgeous]

32.   they let us die "taking a pillow"
        never owners of own illusion
        brave but wasted or free and asleep
        Orion's noose around each fugitive-hero

33.   in the shade of a seed the government speaks
        [dismemberment of the fittest]
        [mimesis revoked]
        is this what a dull sun finds wanting

34.   to whom it may [undecided]
        the black swan [sunk]
        or a heart by any other [fault]
        [truth not reconciliation]

35.   teach them well [no prisoners]
        [happy vengeance and trampled faith]
        gods are [just men]
        disemboweled by memory

36.   [in] human and [non] exempt
        [are we dead yet?]

37.   black rain-on-rain
[word's lust] paid for servitude
eternity [charmed in love]
to reveal [what has always been known]

38.   being equal [slave-to-slave]
being subordinate [wanting the particulars to be true]
being disarmed [cunning so ask no favor]
being sufficient [for every cause]

39.   the purest music [bow-string drawn across skin]
a fugitive childhood [flowered between mouths]
to be free from pain [the book of ravenous cruelty]
but first the known world

40.   [to be] consecrated with one's own blood
or a tongue between thick wet thighs
that pride inconstant a silence uncomposed

41.   two crows scooped mercy's fruit
because we are all
[against our will] the same

42.   [learning to swallow prey alive]
the pinnacle of knowledge
[what a dream foretold]
sublime malnutrition

43.   for fear [for love]
        the sweet of sex
        [a copious evil]
        to make us "free"

44.   so we [eat] what we [see] first
        stagnant eye stuffed down
        every living throat inebriated

45.   at the barricades
        slew every seed-of-seed
        never naked enough

46.   poetry cuts time as
        flowers depopulate a graveyard
        [describe cold water] or
        [the snake that swallowed itself]
        a living tomb [between scream and song]

47.   sophistry in a grain of sand
        [wordgrave like clockwork]
        depravity from a stream

48.   [a threat to the sky]
        [an insult to the winds]
        [a curse to the rains]
        no harm done

49.   great empty country
      , [a sky without camouflage]
        happiness awash
        [stick for stone for broken bone]

50.   on an island in the middle
        of a river in the middle
        of a forest stacked like pages
        in a fire smoky with surprises

51.   skull of the world
        breathing through straw or
        old intestines [incontinent]

52.   if the conquered are
        no longer themselves
        what have [you]
        made [us]

53.   stone fence cut river
        black as sun in cloud face
        outer's ever and lesser heart
        lost at play in space-less space

54.   desire may flinch in effigy
        but faith eats its dead
        in order to live forever

55.   [rain on the siege machine]
        the army on its back
        drinking blood from the sky
        all day play on whistle
        carved from a virgin's thigh

56.   the romance of nations
        only exists in confession
        one to denounce
        one to execute

57.   god surrendered to
        the threat which saved Islam
        from the smell of Europe
        [a reader born blind]
        [a map of meanings]

58.   the king is [just data]
        long live [the murderer]
        [a saint] pledged to
        terror [without dogma]
        perfect states of [carrion] mind

59.   men and women [!] from
        the vanishing lake [our passion]
        mount your [one-way commitment]
        and ride up from hell

60.   ashes of paradise
        a scorching tooth
        [slippery in heaven]
        [leaden on earth]

61.   imagine springtime denied by vice
        spit into the face of history's sleepy grin

62.   a man lying to men laughing
        then slaughtering every living thing within the walls
        never touching the property of the dead

63.   lyricist warrior omnivore cashier godhead

64.   as if the world accumulated a future
        of perfumed merchandise and interchangeable fates
        superimposed on a body so transparent and plentiful

65.   how do they survive
        by gift or by conquest
        and make the gift of death
        lavish and holy

66.   the box of the world split open
        and every god-given purpose
        chose the lesser of one

67.   [a pledge to the rains of sexual gratification]
        what is necessary in peace and bondage
        [to gain success or become a threat]
        that all things profit from themselves alone

68.   to be bride to an enemy
to ride spirit horse in wet sand
to observe the observer
[back into the ground]

69.   as if by thinking could forget anarchy
[or the howls of migrating fish]

70.   build bridges fix roads pardon the condemned
still the poor are born naked [stupid with magic]

71.   encircled a city called [unknown]
fire is the motor of history
[what a suffix oppresses]

72.   now left with these mudmen orphans
public gods fucked what moved
each self-hood on fertile parade
nympho's promise [ready-to-wear]

73.   what is hope without doubt
[to die among privilege]
[to endure the middle of the day]

74.   after seven days
puddled to glue
how much more could be pleasured
by whatever one returns to

75.   [removed for study]
        a constellation knotted by
        holes between bodies
        one can never escape

76.   from the book of doubles
        made a garland noose
        from backbone
        a wish [k]not

77.   west [safe]
        east [safe]
        even mortality
        [wasteful delight]

78.   at moment of own release
        [standing in a word]
        [astride a hollow drum]
        perfected [ignorance]

Pre-Science

nothing returns

only
accumulates

—Tracy Grinnell

I.   This is the person who is not a person.
           This is the world that is not a body.

       Halt and be cognized.
           Origin means entitlement.

       The goal of power is to destroy.
           Of course, innocence is just the bait.

II.   Human stream, human clot.
           No form uncontained.

       A house is not a bone.
           More like a lie in unison.

       Let a thousand blanks bloom.
           Beggars can't be democrats.

III.   So what to tell the machine?
              Repression. Entertainment. Repression.

           Silence has misunderstood loyalty.
              Blessed be the barren.

             Give them their fear, their daily womb.
                 But never hesitate to sacrifice others.

IV.   This is why they invented imagination.
              And those semi-precious death camps.

           "Because they can."
              Memory is not free.

             So if a tree falls. . .
              Next witness.

V.   There are never enough ideas to go around.
              Then the clock stops.

           Fact: survival trumps admin.
              Fact: words colonize air.

           Nature seeks content.
              Fate wants to be a bank.

VI.   Every desire produces a counter-desire.
            As in beauty's lifelikeness.

        Optimism simulates orgasm.
            The hidden cost is the unit price.

        All for one and one more later.
            What else could an electorate ask for?

VII.   This is that which is excepted.
            Law makes the law.

        Like that iceberg metaphor.
            Another pyramid scheme in a Petri dish.

        To populate the future,
            One must first reverse it.

VIII.   Man is the "_____" animal.
            Liberation means new forms of fear.

        But these graves won't protect anyone
            When it's time to testify.

        Promises are made to be token.
            The original perjures itself on faith.

IX.   History comes from dislocated pattern recognition.
          But what if they step into a river that is not moving.

          Predestination talks the talk.
             But as it turns out, now was never here.

          Idealism will find a new enemy.
             Self-interest doesn't know any better.

X.   Coincidence abhors change.
          Fidelity must be its own reward.

          Do neurons eat other neurons?
             So much for immunity on Sunday.

          Go with God.
             Take your stuff.

XI.   A nude window carved the air.
          Is there a surcharge on wish-fulfillment?

          Solids aspire to liquid lives,
             A sphere that is all equator.

          To write is to hide.
             Retreat. Rescue. Retreat.

XII.   The thinkable choked on its tongue.
           One more self-perpetuating sundial.

        Without surveillance, everyone
           Would be the same.

        Dust of a golem.
           Coffin in a cloud.

XIII.   One bird, one stone.
           There's no limit to limits.

        Invisible thus expendable.
           Time is money left behind.

        One ever intends the other.
           Forever, before it's too late.

Last Man Standing

A Shepherd's Calendar

I'm the one who's
running out

and then

time's
on its own

—Keith Waldrop

hello mutant
welcome back

horses are falling
birds freeze under the bed

god told the first lie
ends-over-means

excess is not a weakness

•

the distance between
seeing and thinking
is everything else

what we hated
was expression

•

in a moment of suspicion we identified the ideal: every
permutation a winner, pornography like poetry but without
illusions

•

generation to generation
the problem remains

who is dead
and who isn't

•

hope's alibi:
continuous war

that which cannot endure
the labor of longing

because if a slave wants for nothing...

•

conjugated by idolatry
intoxicated by simulacra
seduced by mediocrity
acquitted by patricide
depopulated by appetite
dessicated by confidence

•

the sign said "action not knowledge" but how many words does
it take to change the light at the end of the tunnel and are we
even responsible for content just as "the beginning" has no
beginning and death has failed to make a difference

•

wherever we are going
our enemies get there first

speak of the devil...
adaptation headed for higher ground

●

creation doesn't feel

●

what worth an heir deceived
by improbable static feasts
remote and franchised
to abide by horror's peace

●

then, as they say, "the light fails"
simplicity celebrates erasure
resurrection demands material proof
one infinitesimal revenge
after another

●

self-preservation is
suicide's disguise

crime never could
keep a secret

dawn in the crematorium window
appearance fashions its own order

let's fight fire with fire
nature deserves to fail

•

copernicus built the bomb that defined us

but can defeat be endless and successful

one sees the occasional symmetry

•

what would it be like
to defend a "self"

or to begin every journey
anticipating the moment of return

"I'm not dead yet"
so much for echoes

•

then the stories came out to meet us as if
the hypnotic was inseparable from its symbols
and beauty exhaled a copy of beauty

●

the persecuted persecuted
the hordes civilized

a prostitute promised justice
a cannibal promised equality

the old world conquered difference
the new world memorialized amnesia

posterity intoxicated remorse
immortality rehabilitated every disease

●

orthodoxy was voluntary
they made the future safe for fear
"no exceptions"

●

without warning the herds started flowing backwards from
incubator to wilderness perhaps attracted by the scent of a new
genome or commands from an uninterruptible language in
which no regret is left unspoken and democracy adores a mute
witness

●

truth means "to wallow on the brink of conviction"

as if you were the last person alive

●

what if the primordial
had been impotent and
evolution fermented from
extinction to fetal slime

●

fog in fog
then daylight

each indigenous pseudonym
as good as it gets

●

that which outlives contemplation
wakes to exploit another day

blood worms thicken water
rain climbs the walls

ambition emptied the lounge while
the muse searched unclaimed baggage

the tarmac had been painted
"this is the past — start somewhere else"

•

today needed a better alternative to temptation's consequences
and epilogue in precedence that is something worth dying for all
over again

•

self-serve philosophy taught us
nostalgia as identification logic

plagiarism's loving song
of perfection in absentia

•

universal so familiar
universal so authentic
universal so idolized
universal so immortal
universal so unendurable

•

such are the affairs of state:
every morning an emancipated fastlessness
every evening the ambiguous constellation

"pay me now or pay me later"

•

then the sun came out and changed the rules
no light but shadow's generous inadequacy

an inconsolable reflex, an unspeakable ecstasy
can we be reborn without science

•

the horizon is made of property
industry fills silence with sentiment

did you enjoy your visit to the slaughterhouse
abscess marks the spot

•

they kept writing
looking
for "the other"
but there was
no other

•

first and last
the milk of waste

what would make the next
five minutes worth living

•

desire invented the adjectival mind
even if we are not *not here*
the absolute fails us every time

mimicry in zenith
ill-ripened magnificence

impasse
precedes judgment

the best stories end
with contempt

•

semen written on the tree of babel:
does image imply meaning

•

had to be equal to have a motive
had to be subverted to have a footing
had to be claimed to have a story
had to be preserved to have an asylum
had to be impregnated to have
nothing left to deceive

•

faith chose death by immolation
love chose death by garrote
perhaps we should make things simpler
is the apocalypse today or tomorrow

•

so what did they learn by
subject-object deification?

"good weapons come in small packages"
"don't talk to the valuables"

but in the long history of the lie
no one has ever lost any money

•

there are two kinds of people

the slain, a vessel for profit
the faithful, their brides unbidden

each cause brings cause into being

•

the function of memory is
to predict not transform
is the pond filled with "wetness"
does "seedless" insinuate "forever"
only the insured believe in authenticity

•

it is tempting to consider the body as beyond dissent, an ache
without form, an economy of scribbles, but can we assume that
the deceased have reached their potential?

•

war loves law
work justifies crime

from all that effortless begetting
never cease to be in flower or fruit

do you resent what does not exist

natural splendor renounced second nature
a museum of broken bottles
a system insinuated by disease
earth gratefully relieved of its sky

•

in geologic time
epistemology means
a sum of none

will trade food
for sleep
mind for matter

•

this is a closed system
to write to fear to await

viscera hung from an icy battery
finally a flag to believe in

•

those multitudes inseparable from those multitudes compro-
mised by those multitudes presiding over those multitudes
blooming among those multitudes bred to become those
multitudes facing towards a sunrise of dead-on-arrival
perpetuity

•

dark stars drowned out the evidence
can a breath talk back to its lung

ethics wants restitution
volunteers line up here

•

countless
whispers
repeat
each life

quick to
forgive
a tyrant or
imposter

•

a civilization is not happy for its own sake

•

the future fits

return to sender

fifty-nine seconds then
end of rehearsal

no baptism for the after-birth
might as well be mortal

•

new survival list
point a to point b

like rats-of-reason
best foot forward

what kills is not dead
faith least of all

•

having eroded having been flayed
having foreseen having been forgotten
having acquiesced having been martyred
having putrefied having been liberated
having exhausted having been exhausted

•

we achieved perfect entropy without the benefit of white space
but the exclusion that had sustained us recut the map into
pockets of resistance each as sterile as the chronicle we had left
behind

●

"hey baby, bring that bleach over here"

●

instinct's mercy
civilized motive

artifice
was never futile

history measured progress in suffering
the firmament rotted daily
ten-out-of-ten means "the public"
imitation cured our premonitions

•

a man who can't express himself
hangs a man who won't expose himself
to a man who would excuse himself
to a man who slowly stones himself

•

symbol obscures symbol

fertility for obliteration
sterility for restitution

belief for secondhand foresight
in the glass eye of the beholder

•

gravity self-fulfilled
the obligation of
a manifest horizon

to prove existence requires
the merciless dementia
of seeing through mirrors

fact invented absence
that euphemism for
each necessary evil

•

shouldn't we be free by now

•

would a benevolent god have sterilized himself

if you need to ask, don't bother

twilight fears the imagination

find the word for "intercourse"
in the word for "elsewhere"

•

remember that misinformation about the eternal flame of spirit's
naked will domesticating every seed-of-doubt and harnessing
the tyranny of quote time-and-space unquote

•

how to recognize authentic parasites
how to resist the indecent affirmation
how to betray false-positive ecstasies
how to succumb to defected inspiration
how to defect to the threshold of regret

•

so escaped from exile like
Oedipus in a hole and recited
"whose dystopia this is I think I know. . ."

or like a piano on a railroad crossing
conscience left to its own devices sings
"we have nothing to fail but failure itself"

•

note to next world
abundance
obvious mistake

lapwings and ravens fight for low ground
the unfruited tree indefensible at last
can a star curse the sky

•

in lust only one thing matters
to do one's duty from behalf to remorse

thought stinks from the foot

the next life awakened by
an amnesty untempted

•

let x equal y
in suspended obsession

a curiosity lifeless and
unencumbered

•

then to exalt an abstinence replete
vegetal mineral viral

accept that your soul
has already been sold

wind rhymes the silence
that melody of decomposition
which flatters the flesh

•

the advance of age
the age of consumption
the consumption of artifice
the artifice of refuge
the refuge of simulacra
the simulacra of comfort
the comfort of futility
the futility of habit
the habit of advance

•

hard-wired to look for patterns as if one could unwitness the
question and the question of the question in conclusion in vitro
incarnate inexcusable

snow noise last defense
friendly fire and light desecration
one more lifetime without regret

•

fifty-fifty
perjury

camouflaged as
survival instinct

OK fiction
this is what happens

what if one knew
the outcome

of every event
in advance

Loose Canons

To remember everything is a form of madness.

—Brian Friel

RHYME

Yesterday, forgot the world but
someone spoke a language with
only three words: *door, war* and ____.

Today wrote *door* on the door
then locked every door which
made another door necessary.

Tomorrow we will take a photograph
in which the freedom fighters won't
recognize themselves among the oppressed.

But was that a breath or a blank
where a person could write a person
and there was no one left to erase it?

ALIVE AS YOU OR

"I dreamed I saw St. Augustine"
Walking through solid rock
Where an empty space used to be.

He was singing: "A mind
Is a theory of what we know
We don't know."

Patrons enter here: one more
Route to a detour to a "closed-
for-the-season" sign.

The power of identity
Is the choice to identify.
Vanity makes no commitments.

NEVERLAND

for Bob Rizzo

If you're happy and you know it
Does potential trump consequence?
Not if the DNA doesn't match.

The absence of a state
Makes it possible to not exist.
Just press enter.

There is no "team" in "I":
Curiosity kills the cure
By cause and defect.

So when Mr. Tomorrow says
"Go Jump off a bridge"
Natural Selection gets a new career.

ORPHEUS

for Barrett Price

Mounds of sugar drifted across the sunset
While on the beach refugees sang
"Purple haze gets in my eyes."

The night is young, reasoned epilepsy
But it's already too late to quit without
Acknowledging everything we know is wrong.

Does eternity have a strategy in mind?
You'll need an army of grave robbers
To get that egg back into its shell.

Then they paddle back to the mainland
Chanting "denial precedes invention".
There's no public as useless as self-reflection.

MAMMAL JINX

for Charlotte Meehan

In America, the professional talks
For the parent who puts food
Under the table and vice versa.

Collective responsibility sets limits
To the big fish/little fish metaphor:
Are we civilians or are we men?

Contrary to superstition
Zero is not an omission but
The best of the best we can do.

As in those old suicide songs
The last question implies its own answer
And everyone knows what honesty pays.

CHARLEMAGNE

for Mary Beath

Found chewed in birch bark:
"Don't hunt my alibi and I
Won't compute your degree-zero."

Revolution dies hard in the mind
Searching for a perfect rhyme
To catechism without a disclaimer.

An eye first absorbs itself:
The person a person
Will never in fact become.

Found blackened on bone:
"The way of the way is
The most wayless of all."

A KIND OF JOKE

There must be some way out of here
But who would transform a nature
So convenient to repress?

A negative cannot describe itself
Thus the fight-or-flight response
To each fulsome insufficiency.

Was there ever a good time
To be alive, for instance,
When doubt was its own reward?

Survival is the barbarous act:
Nothing left to chance or
The devil the devil doesn't know.

FUGUE

Hey Joe, where are you going
With that half-hour in your hand?
Welcome to philosophy.

Only music defies accumulation.
Faith needs a sewer
Or a fire escape drenched in glue.

Can one practice dying?
"Sure" they said
"This is how it works."

Even uselessness affirmed
Can't replace the pedestal
For what's not there.

MACGUFFIN

Half-noon and the wave arrives:
It's a nine on the DaVinci Scale
The sum-total of well-intended failure.

Then three years in the Kyber Pass
To liberate the Wizard of Oz paradigm
From indiscretion and false patronage.

On the return leg, the band played
"What makes you so special?"
As if we had one life to give over again.

The agenda sells itself:
Freedom requires a patron saint
Like murder or more freedom.

HARDWIRE

Sun comes up, *force majeure.*
It is up to those who sacrifice
To ensure the failure of the future.

They say "the power's on the bottom"
But people don't come wired together
So intolerance must be learned first-hand.

Predictions are only worth what
You pay for them: pain
But no memory of pain.

Now we're waist deep in
The Big Muddy and the old fool says
"Please come again."

CRIME

Dear Prudence, over to you or
Someone who looks like you:
Payback is the status quo.

There are two kinds of people
One universal enemy and just enough
Capital to own all the property.

Now assume the position of
A first-person intransitive and
Conjugate with the interrogative imperative.

In a house made of switches
Tomorrow remains necessary
But insufficient.

A-SUDDEN

When we marched down to Finerio
"Like a lady, like a dove"
Those were symptoms, not selves.

Does horizon imply futurity?
In the minds of the missing
More is the sign for more.

Even if this was a song about sex
Not products, what could be wasted?
True or false: reality wins.

And if we later return from the dead
"Fare thee well" may be too good a word
For the blinding snow, the sum of zeroes.

ANTHEM

for Michael Gizzi

The Beatles said
"Everything is in the future."
That's the price for never making a mistake.

But the next day it rained
Making the furniture worthless
And the inevitable impossible again.

Forty years later, it's another Monday
Another argument against motion:
More work, less shoplifting.

"Good luck" they said at the end
"The world deserves vengeance."
Maybe failure is not the problem.

ABOUT THE AUTHOR

Craig Watson grew up in the middle of the 20th Century in New England and New York. After a purgatorial high school experience and a more entertaining but generally disappointing college endeavor, he began his real education through other means. His theater career began as a technician since which time he has been a stage manager, managing director, dramaturge, literary manager and producer, among other positions in the performing arts. During a decade with a Fortune 500 technology company, he was a writer, marketing and public relations executive, and strategic planner, managing projects in Europe, South America, Asia, Africa and North America. He has also been a volunteer fire fighter, a visiting professor of poetry and drama at Brown University, Wheaton College and other schools, a U.S. delegate to the International Theater Congress, a small press publisher, a husband and father to three children.

This book was designed and computer typeset by Rosmarie Waldrop in 10 pt. Palatino. Printed on 55 lb. Writers' Natural (an acid-free paper), smyth-sewn and glued into paper covers by McNaughton & Gunn in Saline, Michigan. There are 1000 copies, of which 50 are numbered & signed.